Sacred

Social media tags should be

@thelynetteallen

@awomansblessing & @gatherthewomensistercircle

(thanking you in advance for your shares, likes and photography)

www.awomansblessing.com

DEDICATION

This book is dedicated to some very special women.

Firstly Kim who founded Bali Street Mums, a beautifully small and completely transparent charity. She is an absolute angel for the women and children of Bali. She spends her time walking the streets of the city, finding the children who go missing here due to trafficking, talking to mums and children who appear to be begging and living on the streets. She makes life easier instantly with food, water and offering a safe place to stay. Within hours, they can be at the safehouse, eating good food, playing and working out how they can stay, be educated and find a different way of living and making their own money.

Diandra is by Kim's side. A child Psychologist, she does so much. She runs the counselling sessions, organises the paperwork and background checks to ensure the children are kept as safe as possible. She liaises with families, police and the legal and healthcare system to ensure the children get a childhood and their mothers get access to support.

The women and children who are supported by Bali Street Mums have had little to no free choice in their circumstances but a willingness to trust Kim and her team, means that they can find another way of supporting their families, giving them personal pride, safety and financial independence.

Lynette is the Patron of Bali Street Mums and works closely with them.

Any support you feel called to give is deeply appreciated.
www.balistreetmums.org/donate

GRATITUDE

As always, my love and devotion goes to my husband Mark...my compañero, my love, my heart. Thank you for grabbing my hand and taking me on this wild journey into both our souls. I have deeply appreciated you by my side during this integration and 'slow' of the past two years. A rite of passage for us as individuals and as sacred partners. We travel together.

For Rosi, never would I have imagined when I was 21, that just a few miles away from me, a baby girl was being born and that one day, I would know her to her core, that she would know me as well as I know myself and that she would call me Mama also. I cannot imagine a life without you walking it with me, your love and our connection is sacred to me.

To Livvie, my goodness...my youngest girl, my love dove, my heart.
It is an honour to be your Mama, to see you blossom from toddler to a confident, sassy, cool beauty!Thank you for serving medicine next to me, for holding space with me and reminding me what it is to be truly present both in and out of sacred space. You are already medicine.

And to my mum. You and Dad gave us everything growing up, you both sacrificed so much and I appreciate every single thing. It is because of the grounding you gave us and the secure childhood we had, that I do my job as a wife, mother and medicine woman the way I do, with kindness, gentleness, love and compassion for others - whether I know them or not.

Thank you.

Infuse this book with your energy, hold it close, place it on your altar
and know that having this book in your possession was no coincidence.
Everything is divinely orchestrated.

When you sit to open this book, light a candle, bless your cacao or tea
and drink in the words of the pages you choose.
They were written for this moment.

FORWARD

Ahhh Sacred. Another absolute gem from Lynette. I have been inspired by Lynette's work since stumbling across 'A Woman's Blessing' while working with ceremonial cacao and ritual in my own practices. This book really changed my life! I resonated with the words and Lynette's beautiful spirit in such a way I wanted to share her work as a complement to my own.

When 'HELD' was published, it also deeply resonated with me and my journey.
Now 'Sacred' is here and I am totally loving the journey these books take us on our path to awakening, each one growing with us.

Sacred is reminding me of 'simplicity' and how, with simple ritual, time to ourselves and deep rest, we can all heal on such a deep level. These books have carried me and many of my Radiant Woman Tribe in so many ways. Sacred is here to hold our hands to the next level of our awakening and into a new world of love, ritual and magic.

Sacred is here to remind us of the simple things, to support us in living our best lives, in trust, ease and flow. Let the words on these pages guide you to your next step on this dance we call life.

Andrea Jackson

Radiant Woman Founder, Cacao Ceremony & Circle Trainer,
Spiritdance founder & Trainer, Elemental Yoga Founder & Trainer, Spiritual Mentor & Weaver of a Magical life

WORDS FROM THE ELDER

As a loom holds its thread and weaves its magic into colour, Lynette weaves her magic with her words. Intricately shaping thoughts to understand the essence of her being, she brings you closer to your own awakening heart. Sacred evokes a timeless mysticism of the divine feminine, a rhythm and a dance for the ages. Her words have a familiarity that resonates deeply within, like a beacon of hope for the soul to recognise.

This Medicine Woman, born to hold sacred space, captivates and enthralls your longing for knowledge of ceremony, ritual and ancestral truth. Made clearer by her own walk through sacredness to the divine source, she brings forth from these pages a silent meandering of the self, an introspection of what it means to be you. If you listen carefully you will hear the call.

As I read her words, tears filled my eyes, yes it was me. I recognised myself in these pages. The message was loud and clear. I am not perfect but beautiful and rising.
This is she, this girl, this crone, this feminine, she is SACRED.

Sallie Warman-Watts

Visionary Sage Crone, Cacao Carrier, Seer, Medicine Woman, Gather the Women facilitator

Integration...an expansion, a settling,
a melding and melting of new information with old.
Repatterning for growth.
A rite of passage.
It's Sacred.

TO MY SISTERS

Sometimes there is a bigger calling on your shoulders than you were taught to believe growing up. And when it's time for that calling to be heard, it will feel like a falling apart, a destruction, a swallowing up and a disintegration - a smothering of your most vital signs.

It will not feel fair, it will challenge every single one of your beliefs. Your identity will be questioned and it will pull you so far under the earth, you will have no human understanding of how to climb out.

And then...your fiercest warrior woman will emerge.

She will rise from the depths of your solar plexus and she will use her voice, you will feel her fire and she will cast her spells and weave her magic with you. Because there is always bigger calling on your shoulders, because you will have no choice, because you will learn to swim in riptides, because you will know deep in your DNA that you were always growing in order to be re-birthed.

And one day...when your warrior settles and relaxes alongside you, knowing she now has a voice and is free to use it when called, the angels that brought you to the surface for air when you needed to breathe, your ancestors, the witches of your past and the crones who walked before you, will wash you clean, wipe your cuts and you will bathe in your lightness.

Your grace, your compassion and your gentle heart will be swaddled in love and you will understand why.

You will see your journey from the place of the girl you used to be, the woman you are now and the woman you are still yet to become. There will be no tears or grief in the end, just a stable knowing and calm.

You will know exactly who you are. And that will have been the whole point.

THE THREE ASPECTS

To the girls we used to be, we give great thanks
To the women we are now, we give great thanks
To the women we are yet to become, we give great thanks
A'ho

1

Sitting in silence,
she watched her melt thought forms and settle energies,
understanding completely,
that she was forming the foundations
on which the woman she was yet to become would dance.

2

And she noticed.
She noticed everything...
how she responded, her words, her actions, her moods...
that beautiful little soul.
Taking her lead and her confidence,
her care-free step and her swagger,
dancing and copying and loving and liking.
Swishing and swirling and turning.
She was reaching for the stars all on her very own.

3

The time for everything she wanted was right now.
She chose everything carefully...her words,
her vibe, the company she kept and how she blessed the earth.
To take each step purposely felt like walking on fresh air.

4

Her tension had dissipated into the ether,
her confusion had blown away on the wind,
her sadness had trickled into a stream at her feet.
Staring at the heavens,
feeling the cool of the earth,
she knew that the sweetness of her soul was all that remained.

5

She had learned
that words topple easily,
that there's no real need for struggle,
that balance is a universal law
and she only made things worse by spinning.
Swirling dervishes needed no more fire,
she could be ether and wind and water too,
but earth was really her friend.

6

She watched them read her words,
holding them to their hearts,
women around fires and candles
early in the mornings and late into the nights,
across the globe,
women found them.

Like secret letters written just for them,
fate or wishful thinking had led them somehow
and as their fingers toyed with pages,
intuitive questions so carefully chosen,
the words and phrases they needed
fell onto their hearts as tears fell on the page.

And when they found HER
and mirrored those words straight back,
delicious echoes of deep nights with madre caught her breath.
Precious reminders of circles and sisters and plants and silent tears,
she held her breath at the cycle of love.
A calling back to remind her, she loved it when they read her words.

7

She walked because they walked,
born into the soles of the greatest,
strongest women who had walked the earth before her.
Singing and chanting and knowing what to do with plants,
they brewed herbs and medicines in circle with others,
marked lines in the sand,
howled at the moon and cried buckets on the shores of their lands.
They broke and disintegrated and fell
and then re-built themselves with nothing
but spirit and a ferocious warrior heart that said,
“I’m standing and I will be seen once more”.
She honours them every time she drinks,
She remembers them every time she gathers
and everytime she feels the pull of the moon and the sun grazes on her skin, she smiles.
For they were the fire starters,
the witches and the wise ones and they lived and survived for her.

8

She had plans
and she cancelled
and she held her solar plexus with her palm.
Her body sighed with deep, deep gratitude.

9

An understanding of her pain was settling now,
those moments of heart-crushing gulps and stifled sobs,
she knew them intimately and loved them now,
for they were nothing but passing shadows.
And when she kissed their foreheads and held their hands,
years of broken soil and rubble sifted through her fingers like sand.
Fear of drowning and separation and tears on little faces had destroyed her faith, but now, to be clear,
to feel stability and talk of nothing but holding hands and goodnight kisses, meant she was walking on
the softest clay in the coolest streams.
Released and replenished, she was understanding pain now.

10

The calling of the child, the woman and the wiser self.
Separately so familiar, together for the first time.
The child at her feet and the elder opposite them both,
she blessed them with holy water,
placed thumb prints on third eyes,
whispered gentleness in a language unknown while smiling
through kind, watery and elderly eyes.
Cycles and rhythms, wild women calling,
ancient voices and deep caverns of magical medicine.
Worlds collided in these moments and there was no such thing as time.

11

She will not cut her hair,
she will not lower her vibration,
she will not be rushed, poked, moved or shifted from Source.
She knows too much and she admired her for that.

12

Every stride was pressing deeply on new earth now,
making impressions where future women may choose to tread.
Drums being carried, bare feet on moss,
the whole earth felt like home now,
exactly where she had dreamed of being all along.

13

Her rise was never in question,
it was her fall that she'd feared.
Just desperate not to feel that grief and loss,
to have and to hold together the smaller parts of her that wouldn't understand.
She just didn't want to have to do that,
to immerse herself in water that deep.
And while she had no answers,
she knew that time would move them all
and that her rise was never in question.

14

He'd floated away out of her cosmic field,
a distant someone who'd once lit her path,
separated now by the gravitational pull of different solar systems.
And actually that was ok.

15

So tempted with all of her being,
my, my the pull and the draw almost too strong to bear,
she took it back to her stick,
held it and spoke of the very blessings she wanted to nourish instead.
Her elder appearing by her side, she held her hand
and nothing more needed to be said.

16

What she adored most was his weight on her,
his fingers, his grip, his focus and his dedication.
Lips parting and meeting, the smell of his skin and the arch of her back,
that's what she adored most.

17

And she marked her sacred stick.
Three lines.
Stability, emotional presence and groundedness.
Then she blessed it with magic and cacao and spells
and those were the waters of the mornings she now swam in.

18

All wide open,
losing herself to the earth,
she was now the foundation
and the wind blew straight through her hair.

19

She took her stick and dug it down deep into the ground.
Staking a claim.
Blessing the energies that ran through it,
setting intentions and asking permission to do her work with ancient gods.
Dressed in cotton with priests of the past, it was done.
She could move.

20

The mother archetype ran so strongly through her.
Standing between her smallest self and a lifetime of seismic tremors,
sleeping peacefully and so completely unaware how she had just been saved,
there was only one aspect who needed to know
and she was the woman she was now.

21

Learning what was hers and what wasn't,
wrapped in a towel, wiping eyes,
tears and heaviness and weight too heavy by far,
with one deep sigh she stopped.
That sadness wasn't hers, it didn't belong to her at all.
So with compassion and crystal blessings,
she delicately handed it back in time to be dissolved with ancient energy, where it belonged.

22

The unease of something hung around her aura.
She didn't quite have a sense of it...
anxiety, sadness, unease, distaste, misalignment...and then she found it.
Fear.
An old pattern, an old feeling resurrected.
And resurrected she determined it would be.
This time, it would be honoured.
This time she would remember she wasn't responsible for anyone else's feelings.
This time she knew it was medicine,
her only job to hold a sacred container for it to breathe and release.

23

'Medicine is nature' she heard.

'and nature is connection' she was told.

Sacred herbs, shamanic tools, ancient whispers and voices from the past relieved her of overwhelm and brought her right back to the sound of the wind.

24

Moving forward and letting it go she knew,
wasn't about letting time simply run under her feet.
Time hadn't done a damn thing to soothe her heart.
Instead, she'd had to focus on her balance.
Instead, she'd had to dedicate herself to finding stillness.
Past courage and through resilience,
finally into breathing the freshest coolest air she could sense
and then her pain sank deep into the ground.

25

Standing in the crashing waves,
holding her drum to the gods of the oceans,
offering herself and her spells,
they took her breath away and replaced it with bliss.
Vital energy rushing through her veins, she hollered so they could hear.
Every woman, calling them to gather, ancient DNA, she'd held them a thousand times before
and today, they would remember.

26

She released him,
in every sense,
relieved and received,
without control and in surrender,
with her highest vibration
and the divine feminine erupting precious essence,
she released.

27

Sanctuary and sacred gems had been found.
Rubies and crystals rested on the softest moss floors of the caves
she'd wandered aimlessly through on long, torturous, sleepless nights.
Fires had licked at her ankles during witching hours past,
lashing out to shout that all she wanted was to devote time to herself.
And with the low morning sun, it was their embers that revealed those sparkly stones.
Holding them to her lips, laying down on that moss,
she curled up for privacy, solitude and the deepest, deepest rest.

28

The warrior, born of the night.
She'd guided her soul through dark stairways and long halls
with a footstep rhythm so completely sturdy and firm
that it had wiped all doubt clean away.

29

In the quietening of her own internal storms,
she reclaimed ancient cellular memory.
And with it...she'd called in the seer,
the witch and the clairvoyant.

30

Everything about her was gentle to the core,
gentle in her spirit and divine femininity,
treading the earth softly, leaving feathers and shells where she went.
She summoned the kind of peace that only angels dusted with.
And she loved her dearly.

31

Feeling all the lives she'd lived,
all those women,
she felt them step forward,
joining her in her medicine,
like it was their time again, as well as hers.

32

She called upon the women around her and over the oceans
to rise up and be seen,
to hold a sacred circle for their sisters,
to be wise and trust their knowing.
She had their back and she asked them for theirs.

33

It was a complete divinely orchestrated rebuild from a cellular level upwards.
Cellular vibration,ethereal knowing, the melting of everything human.
A slow and torturous disintegration of beliefs
about herself, her role, her marriage, her heart.
And now she could feel the completeness of those cells,
the renewal of clear beliefs that formed solid ground.
Ground on which she could build.
And that was exactly her intention.

34

She gently guided little feet and dripping eyes in the middle of the night to her altar.
Sitting her down on a cushion and giving her the most important job of lighting the candle.
As strength was mustered and focus was found,
a candle shone bright, palo santo was burned.
Talk was quiet and hushed, of sticks and stones
and ocean-washed-up-gems that gathered in that place.
Bells tinkled and the sounds of Tibet were heard.
Smiles and dry eyes lit that space and guided them gently back to bed.

35

As she lay in bed, the sun squeezing through the curtains, she felt them.
Little fairies streaming in, finding her heart,
delicately paying close attention to her remaining scars.
Tiny flutters as fairy stitches with invisible thread melted the final marks and gaps.
She hadn't quite realised this phase was coming to a close
but as water spilled over her head, they anointed her with rose oil and sage.
She had done it, every single part.
She had blindly felt her way through and now the light had arrived.
Threads delicately being weaved through her essence by tiny beings.
She breathed in thanks.

36

'It ended for a reason',
she felt a little better when she heard that.

37

To just sit back, with a cup of tea,
to just allow all the feelings to slide off her shoulders,
meant her heart didn't have to carry so much.
And then she felt almost weightless with relief, after a process of such undoing,
she was rather enjoying the feeling of being put back together again.
Her realisation that the major plan she had for herself
was the one thing she'd been torturing herself with, was a revelation
and the relief she felt, to be able to call this place home, was unimaginable.

38

Sacred union she realised wasn't packaged in neat little brown paper parcels,
it was messy and flirtatious and wild and risky
and each union provided the heart, served the soul,
gifting the sensual and the sexual,
the 'nearly there' and the whole damn nine yards.
Sacred union was the most precious gift to her feminine
and she was completely open.

39

She'd chosen to walk on the earth the same time as he did
and for that, she was eternally grateful.

40

She unbound her feet and a cool breeze washed them as they stretched.
With unspoken permission, she was free.
Sovereignty had been granted.
Her stick had bore witness.
And her freedom no longer ended where her ancestors feared to tread.

41

Something healed inside her that day, as she sat on her mat, floating,
aware that her heart had just been flung open and washed with fresh air.
Her wiser self had offered the most beautiful of blessings and she was eternally grateful.

42

Daughters and mothers, guides and medicine holders,
they'd take themselves off to rest, for silent relief and holy self blessings.
Silent pathways, life-enriching waterfalls,
nourishment they could swim in and ground that would hold them.
She knew this had been her past,
she brought it into this lifetime
and her future self washed her with gratitude.

43

Turmeric lattes and coconut skin, ayurvedic ancients and aztec cacao.
Conversations with Source let her know,
the world would turn by itself and absolutely nothing was required of her.

44

And she remembered that today,
she had everything she'd once wished for
and that touched her heart.

45

When the time came to push for the light, oh she would absolutely know.
And nothing would stop her.
It would seem like the most obvious move in the world.
So to pass the time, she just counted the stars, pushed her seeds deep into the earth
and watered them with spells and medicine and smoke.
Whispers on the wind always found their way home.

46

And with beginnings came endings.
Sometimes she knew which was which and sometimes she had no idea at all.
Neither was she meant to.
For spirit was holding her, in tune with her
and in a complete cycle with her... the beginning, the journey and the end.
And she was still very much on the journey.

47

She let her blood out onto the earth,
expelling all her energy,
releasing her waters and flow into the cycle of life.
With the fire of her feminine flow,
she peaked and purged,
flowering and blooming
and sending her love in ritual.

48

With closed eyes and cacao in her hands she entered her aura,
the delicate sphere just beyond her physical.
She felt the need to gather her power from the edges of her being
and sweep it back into her heart.
Visiting the places and people she had given her power to,
she respectfully stood before them and summoned it straight back.
Every. Single. Grain.

49

The girl she used to be had played on the surface,
seen magic in the rivers,
pulled stars from the sky
and danced with the spirits just for fun.
The woman she grew into held her breath and dove into the underworld,
smouldering, smelting, gripping and clawing for air,
lost in caves of confusion for more days than she could count.
She'd been placed there to ferment, to simmer, to burn,
to incinerate what she'd been fed.
And when the woman she had become pushed through the earth's
crust, little girls flocked to play with her magic,
to jump and steal the stars she placed in the sky
and to watch in awe as she led that dance
with the spirits of every woman she'd ever been.

50

She'd checked every single time, every single decision, every single feeling.

She had checked.

And she could not have played her hand any differently.

51

With deep cuts in her womb healing over,
she started to realise,
she could soften,
she could soften,
she could soften.

52

So many more hills, lakes and rivers to cross.
So many ravines and cracks yet to jump.
But she appreciated what it had taken to get here.
Tears, laughter, darkness and light,
sobriety, faith and warm shards of light to breathe in.
It had taken a thousand flat whites,
soft blankets and deep conversations with love.
It had taken journalling, raucous laughter,
presence, plant medicine, song,
ceremony, drumming and ritual.
It had taken alone time and talking time,
special friendships spanning the globe,
invisible love and softness from so many special beings.
People had shone light into her heart at the perfect time without even knowing.
Eternity would not be able to thank them all.

53

In her silence she explored so much,
entertaining every single sacred thought,
dancing in delicious, yoni-melting gloriously delirious, wild and wondrous love
and licking it up - very, very slowly.

54

Expansion was always and absolutely a part of her existence.
Never in her whole life had she NOT seen and felt it arrive.
Expansion in breath, ideas, opportunities, love, faith and friends.
Expansion was everything and every path led her straight to it.

55

She knew that when she was ready,
it would all line up
and so much was already in view.

56

She gave them everything she had,
without being depleted,
just with love and with care and by knowing that she was valuable.

57

She always accepted the dark as a part of her
but she chose to look at the glitter paved pathway instead.

58

When every step was a prayer.
When every movement was an acknowledgement.
When every token was an appreciation.
She took steps consciously,
she breathed with thought
and she prepared her Self for love.

59

She was smiling as she inhaled the freshness of her discovery.
The disconnection, the holes and the gaps, she'd tried to fill, she now owned as hers.
To let that go gave her the freedom to find her path, to stand strong on her own,
knowing that to call her future self in, was to invite this growth.
Learning to transform pain into independence, sturdiness and discernment,
she was the woman she was yet to become.

60

Holding little hands, lighting sage and
singing mantras into the night ...that's what delighted her soul.

61

Peace.

Recovery and rest.

Nothing more.

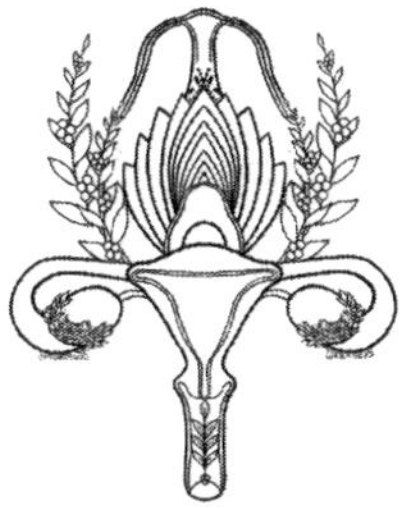

62

And as she sat and she spoke,
telling stories of what brought her through.
She spoke of her deep trust that the essential elements of her,
would be the same elements that would bring her sisters through too.
It wasn't her job to participate in their finding,
just simply to live as she was called to.
To tell her story with love and to trust completely in Source.
Universal forces and planetary guidance would deliver every woman back to her Self.

63

She waited.
It always came.
The plan.
The download.
Falling into the gaps.
She didn't need to do too much.
Just enjoy the moment.
The quiet, the sun, her breath and her cacao.
There would be no stopping her once the plan became clear.
So for now, she rested and listened and moved only towards the light.

64

With her hand on her heart and her eyes closed,
she held the air in her lungs just a little too long,
a teeny slither of pain ran through her.
And it was teeny.
And she was resigned.
But even so, her heart and her breath still admitted it was there.

65

Caught somewhere in the middle.
What was most sacred to her, was being denied.
And at the same time her higher self was throwing open the gates for her,
beckoning her forward.
No-one could ever hold her back, she knew that.
So why was she fighting for breath?

66

So many ideas flew around her mind,
some like birds and fairies and sparkles on the wind,
some like demons and disasters and black figures waiting in the wings.
Black witches had always filled her childhood dreams,
she had worked hard to run away and hide
but they always returned and today she faced them.

67

And it suddenly dawned on her,
that the biggest shift of all
had happened when she had taken the first step.
And even though the direction of that initial step had been off-centre to say the least,
she had taken it.
And there her journey began.

68

Heart held. Closed eyes. Tears streaming. Movement began.

69

'You do you' she said
as she laughed and tossed her hair back and swept out her hand,
a cheeky long laugh falling from her beauty.
'You do you and I'll do me'.
So confident in her own way.
So mature that another has his own way.
'You do you' she laughed,
'and I'll do me'.

70

Orbs and stardust surrounded her.
Light beams and energy and silver stars so bright they almost blinded her.
She knew her own heart.
She knew the power of her own light.
And she wielded it with courage and thoughtful words.
A priestess, a warrior, a maiden, a crone.
She took those footsteps with great care.

71

Freedom, strength and trust.
She lived in those.
And where the cracks drew shards of light,
she chose whether she was bound or not.
Her lineage showed her what bondage truly was.
And this birth had drawn fresh breath for the Maiden, the Mother and the Crone.
Little hands were held, hearts were smudged on coconut wood floors.
Freedom mantras sang through her, carried on the breeze straight to heaven.
And to be clear,
for the Medicine Woman to rise,
she was urged to honour all her aspects.
And they honoured her straight back.

72

Everything came back around in circles.
Everything visited again.
Calm and smiles and blissful mornings and holding hands with sacred candles.
Life flowed like the sea and it was a comfort to contemplate that.

73

Warm rain.
Soft blankets.
Early morning dew.
Warm cacao and a hand to hold. Her heart couldn't
be more full.

74

And every single time it happened, she got stronger and stronger and stronger. Fighting against it dimmed her light...learning to ebb and flow with and bask in the single streak of sovereign she had been handed, brought the priestess in her to the surface. And one day, she would thank the girl she used to be.

75

She kissed her, brought her closer, held her hand and stroked her hair.
She melted her love into her heart and let her know that she was perfect just as she was.

76

There was a version of her just ahead,
giggling and beckoning,
playfully darting in and out of the shadows
of tall forest trees and fresh morning light landing on silver hair.
Her older self, her bare feet dancing on the earth
with the treasure of youth,
wearing the lines of years of smiles,
“This is all ok” she shouted, “this is all completely and utterly and absolutely very ok!”

77

'One sunrise at a time' she thought,
'just one sunrise at time'.

78

"Thank you for being here" she heard,
"you do so much" he paused,
"they sent you because you were the only one who could do this work
and now look at us all, because of you.
You did your work and now we can do ours.
Thank you, rest a little, you're doing so very well".

79

It was new light that told her 'no fear is even necessary',
for everyone on this planet has done things his and her way.
And for those who had dared to leave old ground,
it all worked out so perfectly in so many ways.
And she deeply recognised the need to trust this beautiful, bountiful, great big universe
in every single second and that no fear was even necessary.

80

For the first time,
she really felt she could see into her life,
to understand her and
to be truly thankful for her.

To know that she was chosen for this life and journey,
for this very purpose,
that was new.
And it really meant that she could release the hold.

81

She could see, this was going to be hers.
She had enough information and hindsight and foresight now.
The earth, the wood, the space, there really was nowhere else.
It was her dream and it would find her and that was it.

82

Her voice touched her heart
allowing the tears of relief to cascade down her cheeks.
A reminder that she has a sister, that she is valued,
that she walks the earth in a time where she is appreciated for her gifts
and that if she leaps...the net will always appear.

83

Sacred sticks, dripping with cacao,
she invited them to find the words that would seep into the drift wood and forest falls in their hands.
They drew symbols and hidden meanings,
burning them in deepest reverence to the women they were yet to become.
And while she spoke of the importance of those sacred sticks,
she smiled, because they already knew.

84

Knee deep in crashing waves so loud, so grateful no-one heard her voice.
Private words and feelings, truths and sores being spoken,
splashing her face and neck with crystal clear ocean, salty water meeting hers,
she sobbed for what had been.
And when she was ready and not before,
she returned.

85

Stirring the cauldron with sisters,
spelling and spilling their raw, authentic heart songs.
For birthing mothers, for broken priestesses, for crones who forgot their powers.
Their medicine, potent and from the earth,
made of roots and seeds and leaves and blood.
As medicine women from past lives surrounded them,
pushing their hands into the clay,
lighting up the roots of the trees and the plants the world over,
they were bringing to life and healing the feminine.
This was invitation-only and every woman was there.

86

The masters, the priestess, the gatekeepers and the secret holders she thanked to close,
we're the same ones she'd spoken with the night her forehead was pressed against the earth
and her tears had watered the plants.
Deep gratitude for her life, for her lessons and the woman she had become.

87

She didn't quite know how she'd done it,
come out not just in-tact
but with daughters and sisters and circle and song,
with the masculine and the weight of his chest on hers.
Her only visible scars, worn like the mother.
With softness and a place to breathe comfort and catch tears,
she really had completed her cycle
and now her higher priestess was calling for her strength.

88

Words in the witching hour were cast, hearing the call of the divine in her dreams.

The founding women of the past called and she answered.

She had work to do.

89

Through the eyes of chocolate,
she chanted and sang for her higher self and theirs,
with Shruti and smoke, incense and invocations.
Cacao and her breath opened portals for universes to fall in,
breathing life into dark corners and calling all the angels to come and sit.
All through the eyes of chocolate.

90

Washing shells with little hands,
chit chatting about everything and nothing.
Tied together by the silks on their ankles,
they made sacred moments of peace.
Precious. Nurturing. Blissful.

91

She didn't want to be entered,
she wanted to enter herself.
She wanted solitude and freedom and air
and stand alone, all-by-herself deep, deep consecration.
She honoured and pleasured and poured out the sacred feminine.
If this was life...she remembered why she came.

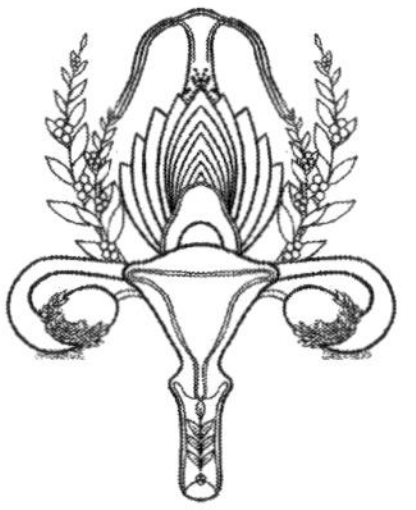

92

A bare stick,
lifted from the bottom of a waterfall
and gifted to her four times with the intention of building dreams.
She marked it with cacao, with burns, with pen and with menstrual blood.
She wound twine around her, whispered to her, blackened her and blessed her with medicine.
She told her a sacred dream, a fresh new one.
Recent, infantile, one that needed nourishment and holding.
One that would birth in its own time.
Like the first trimester when it's so new, you dare not speak it aloud.
And so it was done.

93

Gentle, held, nourished and loved, they giggled and played on their ground,
on their earth, with bare feet and their mother close by.
The happiest of days, the safest of nights.
Heaven on earth.

94

And she gave her pain to the moon,
writing and placing intentions, identifying feelings, wounds and wishes.
Playing with concepts, toying with the future,
lighting smudge to send smoke signals so the moon could hold her pain,
grandmother moon would take it for her.

95

The breaking and the pain,
the intense wounding that collapsed her at her altar,
were the raging fires of the learned collective
and the maidens' saviour being burned.

And even when those fires raged,
she knew they would extinguish and that through death and debris and rubble
and disruption, new life would always grow,
she just had to remind herself that she walked on fertile land.

96

The dream weavers and priestesses,
she knew where they lived.
They lived in temples
with views of mountains and oceans,
they lived in caves with shards of light exposing burning sacred herbs
and they lived in the souls of her dear medicine sisters.
The ones she played with, the ones she served with and the ones she chanted with.
That's where the dream weavers and priestesses lived.
And she was honoured by their presence.

97

The other side of freedom, it seemed, was rejection.
The other side of letting go was the acceptance of absence.
And so...in her freedom, her tears tasted salty and her heart burned a little.
And that was part of the path too.

98

And time would tell,
she had done it before, she knew when the time would be right.
And for now...she planned her blessings.

99

She wished she could hold her heart.
She wished she could whisper in her ear that this was a rite of passage,
that she would breathe again,
that she would feel relief once more and that the sun would find her beautiful face.
She wished she could remind her that THIS is sacred womanhood
and that she would raise beautiful men
who would know how to nurture the feminine
and recognise and revere her strength.
Her angels had a greater path for her than she thought
and she was being handed the keys to her birth rite.
To stand firmly in her own power.
She would feel like she was being held under water for a while
but she would realise in time, that her feet were always planted firmly on the ground.

100

Those candles were her circle of protection,
those women around her, her circle of support.
They promised to hold space for her, to hear her and listen with everything they
had. And the elder among them stopped them and questioned.
Could that really be done?
Could a circle of women really heal the ugly feminine wounds of comparison
and lack and competition and rivalry?
'YES!' they said,
'We are here for you' they said,
And they were.

101

"Tell me where to tread when I am unsure" she whispered.
"Bless me when I cannot bless myself".
She promised to tread gently but purposefully and asked for her lead.
Aware of her presence always,
knowing she had a hand to steady her
and that her future self had her back made her invincible.

102

Space would always be made for her.
She would always land.
Resources would always catch her.
And there really was nothing to do but bask in sunlight patches,
cuddle little children, smile at strangers and thank the stars at night.

103

As she brought them together in sacred circle,
their souls, their spirits and their teachers followed.
To hold their breath as precious and to guide them into their light,
to remind them of that delicate and spacious place between their human and their higher power
as they fell deep into their own silence, was above and beyond magic.
She held space for that silence,
for words to fall,
for thoughts and pictures and memories to release
and for treasured surrender into the medicine.
The breath and the plants held hands and danced the whole time.

104

Sometimes when the panic arrived, she sent it straight down to her feet,
growing roots from her soles, she dissolved it into the earth.
She was always safe there.

105

Closing her eyes to commune with a future soul she didn't know yet,
their hearts settled in time and they began to beat together.

106

She invited her in and she chose to sit close.
Cupping little fingers around hers,
soft cheeks and fairy hair brushing her skin,
"thank you" she whispered.
"I chose you, you know, I chose you".

107

Her mat was her chosen throne,
her kimono...her sacred robes
and cacao...her immaculate medicine.

108

Asking for connection to her higher self was how she started all of her conversations,
in the physical realm and the energetic.
She needed to hear everything.

109

A ritual of awareness.
Sitting alone.
Breathing connection to her spirits and her higher self,
spinning light and warm energy from her crown to her core.
Stillness.
Energising the unseen.
She was clear, a holy channel, she was a carrier.

110

Reaching in to find her heart, she held it in her hands.
Such careful, gentle energy, vibrating it back to life.
Spinning silks of gold, wrapping and winding with prayers and blessings and words and spells.
She closed her eyes, this priestess heals herself.

111

Rose bath milk, ritual touches and warming of skin,
delirious drips of mother nature's finest, orgasmic, self-deepening worship.
This was how she chose her time now.

112

That sacred gateway between her and her, for so many years,
buried and just a feeling of something above...
cracked wide open now and inviting in truths.
Inviting in spirit, hers and others.
Inviting in wisdom, hers and universal.
Inviting in connection,
because it feels so good to be blessed with the soothing energy
that moves mountains and creates world's.
Infinite flow.
Always there.
That sacred gateway between her and her.

113

She made it rain, she watered the earth, she chanted, she stomped and gathered around fires.
She gave offerings to the gods, fanned the flames as she prayed,
brewed medicine for her village and birthed new life safely across worlds.
This was the girl, the woman and the crone she used to be.
The enchantress, the medicine woman and the gift.
Lifetimes of knowing being unearthed in ritual with sisters,
she travelled through time as she gathered the women.

114

Intoxicated by the drummers,
taken under by the plants,
gifted a voice to speak to the spirits,
she cast her magic to far away lands
and they heard every single word.

115

She bowed low to her higher self,
so grateful for the intentions she made before coming into this human experience.
Her connection to higher world's was bursting wide open
and the damns were drenching all she knew.

116

She is meant to be the mystery,
she is meant to be the mover of energies and the dance partner of the spirits.
She is meant to be the secret keeper, the gentle mother, the lover and the wild shaman.
And she's living that really well.

117

Spirit was calling her.
Not the human her but the ancient her.
An artful power and she loved that she could hear.

118

Watching the rise and fall of his chest,
she appreciated the value of his breath more in this moment than ever before.
She would treasure his warmth, his vibrancy and his eyes,
so grateful for every second with him, so so grateful.

119

She really didn’t want to be prodded or poked.
She just needed to be left alone and then she’d find her feet again.

120

To call in her older self,
she leaned into the qualities she loved.
Deep calm, beautiful balance and much, much more laughter and light.
And when she closed her eyes and felt those parts of her opening, she invited her right in close.
She was there.

121

It was on days like these that she had no desire to be anywhere else
but lost in her words and her magic, floating on the breeze of her passions and loves.
She spoke of them often,
invited them in at night
and they lined up in gratitude for her, every single morning.

122

She asked them to look at their feet,
to touch and to hold them,
to remember their journeys,
to remember their steps, their dances, their playfulness and their direction.
For their feet had taken them this far and there was so much more to come.
Together they blessed them and loved them
and covered them with the nourishment of sacred cacao.
Grounded in ritual.
Honoured in ceremony.
Reminded of their right to carry their spells and invited to continue to walk.

123

'How do the women of the world get their spells back?' she asked.
'By listening to their intuition' he replied.

124

She had to write, her life and heart depended on it.
She processed by putting feelings into words and words on screens and pages.
She healed by finding and searching for the perfect expressions
and she will do it until her final day.

125

She realised sometime later that her heart break was her initiation
and that initiations come in so many ways
and that if she had listened to Madre more deeply that night,
her human might have been spared such an arduous, tumultuous, cutting and deeply lonely journey.
But, of course, that was the initiation, a rite of passage in itself.
And one must walk through those underground tunnels on their own.
It's where the feminine goes to rise.
And rise she did.

126

And she held them all like a mother would,
in love, as she listened intently.
She held their secrets,
trusting them to find their strength,
never worried for them or fearful,
their reputations never unravelled but kept in devout
tact. Because she held them as a mother would.
In love and in light and in complete and utter trust.

127

The need to speak, she realised, was about releasing.
And the less she spoke, the more she became the wise elder.
A pot of gold brimming with silver secrets, cherished words and beautiful,
charming memories that the world didn't really need to hear.

128

And she did know.
She knew how to settle herself.
She knew how to be completely calm.
She knew where her soul needed to rest,
on the banks of the rivers and lakes that ran through her veins.
The cliffs and canyons and those diamond studded paths...remember them??
She knew them so well.
The plants had helped her find them.

129

She would sit and stare at that witchy mountain,
waiting and praying for him to come back and for the gap to close.
And for when she could no longer visit
and the miles separated them,
she imprinted the whole valley in her mind.
Just so she could be there.
Closing the gap.
Smiling and remembering her journey.
At the bottom of that beautiful witchy mountain.

130

It was the space in between where the words would drop.
And that's the space she found.
On the days when her body separated from her mind and her mind had nothing in it anymore.
That's the space she found when she went all quiet and distant.
The most peaceful place in her world.
The space in between where the words would drop.

131

Three candles.

For the little girl she used to be, the woman she was now
and the woman she was yet to become.
She always lit three candles now. Since the women had gathered.

132

Before the candles and the rituals and the spells and sticks could work their magic,
she just had to clutch onto the life force of breath with all her might.
And she showed her how.
Placing a hand on her heart.
Holding her head with such deep care,
she sighed an audible sigh so she could follow,
and slowly they breathed together.

133

Fear was insidious, she was once told.
And she never knew what to do with that
until she felt the slathering of it
passed from one to another so damn eloquently.
A silent smearing.
It soaked in so fast, she barely had time to notice.
And while it stayed with her,
spewing black clouds all over her heart and virtually suffocating her,
the foetal position was the only thing that helped.
And even in the pit of that dark black cloud
and even in that hidden child-like pose
she absolutely and unequivocally felt her strength.
She was rising with every single breath.

134

Nothing emptied her full heart of a heavy load faster than her spells.

The written word.

Promises on a page.

Notes to self and love pouring out of every cell.

So much love, so much love, so much love.

135

Walkways of ancient wood, candles and lights and fire so bright,
bare feet being called by that drum.
Medicine women and guides and fairies and elderly witches with kind watery eyes,
ushered them silently into her sacred place to sit and to breathe and to drink.
Oh Medicine. Medicine. Medicine.

136

Slow worship.
Imagining and inspiring visions into life.
Placing sacred hands on hearts,
drinking medicine mindfully,
seeking the holy and the full.
And she opened like a flower drinking from endless water streams deep below the earth.
Slow, slow worship.

137

And even when her heart was heavy,
she looked back on the girl she used to be and loved her so much.
For she had been brave.
She had walked into the unknown.
She had given up everything she owned.
She had said yes, completely sure there had been absolutely no other choice.
And now when she put her hand on her heart,
the woman she was now, could unequivocally say, that even through her tears, this was right.

138

Calming and quietening,
soothing and settling,
softening and stilling,
palms together,
she brought them up to her third eye in reverence and remembrance.
Everything was going to be ok.

139

When she remembered that no decision carried such permanence,
that she could not, at any time of her choosing, change her flowing and feminine mind,
then she allowed her dreams to float on the warmest of currents.

140

And then, on a breath, there was nothing more to say.
She was complete.

'CAUSE I'M POWERFUL

I used to be a girl who was shy,
I used to be a girl who was afraid to say her piece,
then I found my sword of light,
I found my wings,
I saw my light.
I realised I was special,
I realised I was powerful,
I realised I was me,
I realised I was me.
I found myself,
I found a girl who wasn't shy to say her piece,
I found a girl who wasn't afraid
and that girl was me.
After I found my sword of light,
after I found my wings,
after I saw my light,
I realised I was powerful.

I realised that
that girl who was shy,
that girl who was afraid to say her piece,
I realised I had to let her go,
I had to leave her behind
and I had to move on.
And now I've moved on,
and now I'm that girl who's standing in front
of you and she's no longer afraid,
she's no longer shy
because she's me
and...
I'm not afraid,
I'm not shy,
I found my future,
and my future is bright
and my future is light
and my future is me.

Song written by Olivia-Drew Spall, aged 8

GATHER THE WOMEN

Woman of earth, may you be held,
woman of water, may you flow free,
woman of fire, may you shine bright, may you burn all our fears away, woman of air,
may you be blown by the breath of life.
Gather the women,
it's time to step into our power, it's time to rise,
remember the women
silenced merely for being themselves, for being fierce and wild and wise.
Sisters, gather all the parts of you
from all the corners of this beautiful earth
where you have scattered your precious self.
May this song summon
all the sacred parts of you,
the girl you were, the woman you are
and the woman you are yet to become.
Nurture our daughters,
may they understand
the truth of their power
before they come of age.

Nurture our mothers, may they know they are loved
even if they don t know how to reciprocate.
Cherish our grandmothers,
let's all be aligned,
come back to a time
of Sacred Eldership.
Honour our ancestors
by doing the work
and healing our hearts,
we are curing ancestral pain.
Woman of earth, may you be held,
woman of water, may you flow free,
woman of fire, may you shine bright, may you burn all our fears away,
woman of air, may you be blown by the breath of life.

Song written by Abbey Elizabeth Sykes,
written especially for Gather the Women
and gifted as a meditation
to those going through the Gather the Women 2 programme

JOURNALLING PAGES

‘The most powerful statements on the earth’, she said,
‘start with ‘I..’.
They are intentions.
They are spells.
They are bound by universal law.

'I am...'

allowed her to bring herself to presence, to dream herself into being

and to embody every sacred ounce of deep self-love she could find words to describe.

'I will...'

tied reminders to her fingers, adorned her stick with intentions and sent rockets of pure desire up into the stars.

'I will...' she wrote and her heart poured onto the page

'I love...'

She lit a candle and sipped cacao, held her heart and spilled words of love,

filling every corner, writing in circles and bubbles and lines, decorated with flowers and doodles and sacred shapes.

Every single love was described in ink for her to fill herself up on a rainy day.

'I have...'

She couldn't find a better way to appreciate the girl she used to be,

other than by recognising the gifts she'd given the woman she was now.

'I see...'

She saw through the eyes of her wisest self, she saw her future, she saw where she was breaking ground and how she trod on the earth.

She saw her loves, her treasures and the seeds she'd planted. The visible and invisible, in clarity, in depth and in colour.

'I gained...'

oh such thoughtful moments alone with cacao, fairy lights and soft blankets.

Asking source to guide her script...she wrote with her eyes closed.

'I will be...'

Future notes to self, words written on her behalf.

Closing her eyes, she asked for visions to fall onto the page from her future self so far in the distance she could barely sense her.

And yet they came.

'I feel...'

Someone once told her to put her hand on her heart and ask what she felt.

She did and that's how she feels now.

"My time for rebuilding is here
and I'm ready to shed my old skins,
to nurture my heavy,
to lean in, to love and be held.

A new chapter is here.

A story untold.

Unravelling myself, courageous and bold"

Rosi Withers

PRAISE

My greatest and deepest thanks for those who gather,
for those who lead circles and for those who take these words into the centre of their hearts.

A'ho Sisters

“The third in a beautiful trilogy. Lynette's words are filled with magic and strength when pulling together the archetypes of women that live within us. These women are always by our side and can offer strength and advice when we feel we've run out ourselves.

'Sacred' is an enchanting reminder of who resides within”.

Rosi Withers

Wild mama, nurturer of the plants and free spirited fire fuelled lover

“Lynette's words transport me. Her words wrap around me with a warmth and a guided knowing.
They ask me to trust in myself. In my womanhood. In all womanhood, past, present, and future.
Her words hold me in the knowing of sacred energy and as I read, I remember something that I realise
I never really forgot and that is, what it means to be connected to my feminine.
I am so grateful to Lynette for her wisdom, intuition, and guidance.
For her complete connection to that which is sacredly female”.

Nicola Unite

Guider of the breath, counsellor, space holder, cacao carrier and Gather the Women facilitator

“A beautiful guidance for every woman walking her path, to be seen and to be heard just as she is, with love and self acceptance. Sacred is guiding women to stand raw in their own vulnerability, looking past their stories and their wounds, knowing they are on this journey together.
Each one of us holds the key to unlock ancient wisdom that lies deep in our womb,
that we are the sacred medicine to unravel our innate wisdom.
Lynette’s beautiful compilation of her own sacred wisdom unravels the innate wisdom we all hold”.

Jags Kaur

Medicine Woman, Yoni Steam facilitator, Cacao Carrier, Womb Empress, Gather the Women facilitator

"I have worked with A Woman's Blessing and Held every day for many months and they have supported me on a journey from a basic self-care practice to self-love that is deep and enduring. My personal rituals and ceremonies have become sacred and now this book has arrived to help me explore the Sacred.
What is 'Sacred' to me? Each line is beautifully crafted to take me on a journey to discover the answer to that question. Lynette's words make me want to drink cacao, walk in ancient forests, massage my feet and love myself with such depth and honesty. To love every aspect of myself as a mother would and invite other women to do the same. There is magic in these pages and this magic is sacred.
Sacred - a word so loaded with meaning.
My sacred magic lives within me and this book is a portal to the very centre of my sacred self".

Stevie Jane Foster

Cacao Carrier, Medicine Woman, Gather the Women facilitator

"Little did I know that when I grew up, I would discover I was a time traveler, journeying infinite loops.
Inspired by the first in this trilogy, A Woman's Blessing, every one of those words resonated so deeply with me that I went on to join the 'Gather The Women' programme and I journeyed over and over with Ixcacao in my hands.
With all the inspiration and wonders of a little girl, Lynette's latest words give me chills of excitement.
They've given me even more lung capacity to breath it all in, to live my life and to fill myself right up until I spill over.
I've changed forever and I time travel with so much more ease now as I trust in the process every single day.
All because I saw truth within these words.
And so..with Cacao down my fingernails and the cup in my hands, I anoint my feet and I'll be gathering sisters along the way also, waiting with excitement for more words, as we journey back and ahead, towards more of our own answers.
You'll find me, finding Me.
Lynette's words showed me it was all within me".

Katie (KaT) Thomas

Hedgewitch Medicine Woman, Cacao Carrier & Gather the Women facilitator

“Lynette’s words move me in the same way that the poet Rumi’s do.
I know that deep inside me is a resonance which needs to be revealed and brought to consciousness in order for me to fulfill my soul’s purpose, and, for me, the beautiful evocative words in this book are the catalyst for that to happen. The words open my heart and raise my vibration enabling me to truly walk my talk on the sacred path, I’ve walked for many lifetimes.

Sacred is so breathtakingly beautiful to me, evoking an ancient calling of sacred living temples, sacred plants, rituals, dance, priestesses - they reside deep inside me. I‘ve been slowly allowing this ancient calling to rise into consciousness and this book just completed the task in the most intoxicating way. These words evoke my deep reverence for this ancient way of sacred living showing me the path to follow”.

Lesley Readman

Chakra dance facilitator, Cacao carrier and Gather the Women facilitator

"And she was there, holding space for us, to unlock our gifts, to help in releasing our fears and in embracing our secrets in such a gentle way, detached, in sacred silence.

These words came just at the right time, as a pillar of my own growth and my own discovering.

I thank Lynette for teaching me a way to learn more about myself and then be in service for other women as me".

Maila Salmaso

Cacao guardian, earth keeper and Gather the Women facilitator

"Sacred takes us on an even deeper journey into Lynette's magical world.
A wordsmith of our times, magical and profound, all three of these books need to be in the hands of any woman on a journey of Self Love and discovery. Just turn a page and prepare to be deeply moved in both your heart and soul. Thank you once again Lynette.
Beautiful and important work for supporting us all in these exciting and challenging times".

Nicky Hollins

Oh my Goddess Cacao Carrier and Space Holder

"Oh my goodness as I held 'Sacred' in my hands and drank in every word, I could feel my heart beating, my breath deepening and my soul soothing. For me, this time of the menopause is my time to come home to myself, rewrite my story and enjoy every moment of my final chapter.

The words in 'Sacred' are a beautiful guide to hold you by the hand and walk beside you as you hold sacred space for yourself".

Mairi Taylor

Menopause Rockstar, Midlife Coach and Woman's Wellbeing Guide, Gather the Women Facilitator

"Reading Lynette's book felt like a homecoming.
I felt my entire being coming to life reading these words and clarity rising through me.
This book is a must for anyone walking their spiritual path.
Magic does exist and it's in here".

Wakanda Phoenix

Artist, Musician Scientist, Medicine Woman, Daughter of Freya

"Lynette's words spoke to my soul once more. They are truly sacred.
It was as if they were written for me, I feel all who read them will feel the same, for the magic woven within, speaks to the soul. A delightful journey, a mirror into the depths of the longing, the being and the hope, oh the hope it brings, calling me home.
Thank you once again Lynette, you are an inspiration".

Kirsten 'Kimama' Lapping

Energy and Crystal worker, Medicine Woman and Daughter of Freyja

"Deep work requires deep connection…to ourselves, the land we walk upon, the elements and our most divine inner being. Lynette carefully crafts her words and rituals in such a way that those of us who, for a while, or perhaps even since childhood, have lost this connection, are once again able to fall back in love with the parts of ourselves we had forgotten or disowned".

Louise Edwards

Gather the Women facilitator, Dru yoga teacher, Cacao Carrier

"What beautiful words Lynette has used to remind me of the journey I have traveled. Words which have held and nurtured me to be the woman I am".

Suzanne Lister

Women's Health Coach and Gather the Women facilitator

“Lynette’s words are a warm embrace on a cold winter’s night. Channeled directly from the heart, hey touch you in places you thought had no feeling. Sacred is an ode to the importance of ritual as a means to connect with ourselves and access the magic, mystery and wonder of life”.

Abbey Elizabeth Sykes

Cacaoista, Yoga Teacher, Spiritual life coach, Gather the Women Facilitator & Musician

THE TRILOGY

‘A Woman’s Blessing - Nourishment for the rise of the feminine’
was the first written in this trilogy.
'HELD - Guidance for the rise of the feminine' was the second and
'Sacred - Integration for the rise of the feminine' is the third.

This is the journey, a woman's journey, it's your journey.
May it nourish you, guide you and support you in your cohesive and beautiful rising.

GATHER THE WOMEN

- a 22 day immersion

Gather the Women is a 22 day immersion into the 3 aspects of ourselves,
the girls we used to be, the women we are now and the women we are yet to become.

Women across the world from Australia, US, UK, Europe and Asia,
have joined these small (mainly on-line) sister circles.

22 days of cacao ceremonies, ritual, blessings, meditations and rites of passage.

This is not to be undertaken lightly, it's a journey into your Self,
with a small committed group of women all doing their inner work too.

Expect tears, expect laughter, expect to listen to another's story, expect to have your heart touched, expect drop-the-mic moments, expect gushings of love for yourself and every other woman there. Expect peace, expect acceptance and expect to be changed.

Lynette has trained other women to hold their own gatherings also,
so message @gatherthewomensistercircles on instagram for dates of all their gatherings.

GATHER THE WOMEN

- Part 2

And then there's Gather the Women 2...integration and elevation, this is next level.

Advancing your relationship with the woman you are yet to become,
you'll playfully dance with the girl you used to be, listening to the wisdom she offers
and embedding your commitment to honouring the woman you are now.

Plus we introduce our 4th aspect, our higher selves, making a connection to the stream of consciousness we all have access to but so easily forget, mistrust or block. This is the channel where the women we are yet to become speak to us from and this is the channel we will clear, learn to feel the flow in and find our own ways of receiving and sensing clarity beyond just words.

GATHER THE WOMEN FACILITATOR TRAINING IS ALSO AVAILABLE

To be eligible to become a Gather the Women facilitator,
you must first have gone through Gather the Women 1 first.

ABOUT THE AUTHOR

She is the mother archetype with crone energy, a carrier of medicine, a teacher and a harmoniser. She carries no manual or notes but trusts that words will come in the right order, at the right time, to land exactly where they are meant to.

She trusts her loves to find their way, finds new earth to grow in barron cracks and through vines of confusion - she is a weaver and a time traveller, with deep feelings for little hearts who have no concept of their power yet and she stands for them.

She grew strength and calm, yet breathes fire when she needs to and her butterfly wings carry her in circles, pollinating those who sit with her.

She knows growth and is never far from the edge, knowing that the comfort always remains inside and that the woman she is yet to become is always lighting her path. She sees the soles of elderly feet and a dirty trailing white dress climbing over mud and rocks, always way out in front, encouragingly yelling 'You're doing so well, keep going!'.

STAY CLOSE

If you feel the call, join us for your own 22 day Gather the Women immersion.
Instagram your own personal favourite daily passages,
and know that there are a million women behind you, supporting you and feeling your journey...
you are doing so, so well.

We love instagram

@thelynetteallen
@awomansblessing
@gatherthewomensistercircle

and send your appreciation to our medicine sister, tattooist and illustrator @ami_suel

Printed in Great Britain
by Amazon

67872331R00111